Making Your Own

Traditions

by Dette Hunter & Jocelyn Shipley

Traditions Press
Newmarket, Ontario
Canada

With thanks to —

* *John, Chris, Sarah and Mary Hunter*
* *Allan, Brian, Caitlin and Graham Shipley*
* *family and friends*

Who provided inspiration, moral support - and just plain help!

First Printing September 1984
Second Printing October 1984
Third Printing May 1985
Fourth Printing November 1985
Fifth Printing September 1986
Sixth Printing November 1986
Seventh Printing April 1988

Canadian Cataloguing in Publication Data

Hunter, Dette
 Making your own traditions--Christmas

ISBN 09691869-0-8

1. Christmas decorations. 2. Christmas cookery.
3. Handicraft. I. Shipley, Jocelyn
II. Title.

TT900.C4H86 1984   *745.594'1*   *C84-099500-8*

Printed by: *JB Printing Ltd.*
       169 Charlotte St. S.
       Newmarket, Ontario
       L3Y 3S7

Published by: Traditions Press
       125 Arden Ave.
       Newmarket, Ont.
       L3Y 4H7
       (416) 895-2420

Printed in Canada

Preface

*We felt it was about time for a realistic Christmas book for parents, by parents; of fast, easy things to **do**, not worry about! We each have three kids and have created more Christmases than we care to count. Besides getting older we've learned a few things about kids and Christmas.*

Many of the ideas in this book are familiar - they're basic Christmas traditions. The kind of crafts you made as a kid but can't quite remember how the fold goes, the kind of recipes you tuck away then can't find when you want them, the kind of things you phone your sister/neighbor/mother for. They're magical and memorable enough to appeal to both parents and kids. And they work. That's why they've been around so long.

*You can depend on **Making Your Own Traditions** to get you through Christmas merrily every year. And you won't need traditional skills, elaborate techniques, exotic materials or ingredients. We've searched, adapted, and simplified - so you'll have more time to spend with your kids and more time to celebrate Christmas together.*

*When you're overcome by a sudden burst of energy to make something for Christmas, reach for and rely on **Making Your Own Traditions**. Relax about details - most traditions can stand a little ad-libbing. But we think you'll be surprised how well everything in this book turns out, regardless of your age, sex, status or talent. And so will Christmas, when you and your kids are making your own traditions.*

Ages and Stages

We haven't given age ranges because we've only chosen crafts & recipes flexible enough for any or all of the family to do together. But here's a general guide:

* Little kids can do them with help.

* Middle-size kids can do them with semi-supervision.

* Big kids (and middle-age ones) can probably do them without help.

We've found doing **something** for Christmas is the perfect antidote to feeling guilty about all the other things we can't do, and the best remedy for the rising panic that we'll never be ready. It will work for you, too. Many of our crafts and recipes can be made in half an hour and require little or no clean-up, so no matter how busy and hectic your life, or how varied the talents and temperaments of your family, you'll have no trouble finding something that suits.

Projects that traditionally take all day we've put in a separate section, "Special Edition Traditions". But to tempt you to try them, we've broken them down into manageable time chunks you can fit in between loads of laundry or whatever.

To Parents

When you have an overwhelming urge to rush out and put your whole Christmas on charge-x, sit down and remind yourself that making things with your kids produces more than just the finished product. For your kids there is also:

* *The joy of sharing - of being a giver not just a receiver.*

* *An immense satisfaction from creating and completing. (And you can complete the things in this book.)*

* *A rare sense of accomplishment (that T.V. doesn't give) - of being a doer, not a watcher.*

* *Pride in knowing they've really contributed to the family celebrations.*

* *A feeling of control over how and what they celebrate - a glancing poke at that multi-mediated monster - Christmas commercialism.*

* *The mastery of simple skills (manual, artistic, problem-solving) - building blocks of self-confidence and future successes.*

* *The special pleasure of working with you, of sharing your time and attention.*

* *A sense of continuity with the past, of heritage, roots and belonging.*

Contents

Anticipation

Cards & Wrap

Trees & All The Trimmings

Making Gifts

Inside Tips

Cookies - Fast & Festive

Special Edition Traditions

Time-Release Recipes

Atmosphere

Some sayes, that ever 'gainst that Season comes
Wherein our Saviour's Birth is celebrated,
The Bird of Dawning singeth all night long:
And then (they say) no Spirit can walke abroad,
The Nights are wholesome, then no Planets strike:
No Faiery takes, nor Witch hath power to Charme,
So hallowed, and so gracious is the time.

Shakespeare

Anticipation

The whole world is gearing up for Christmas - and all you want to do is watch the first snowflakes fall and savor the delicious anticipation of Christmas coming. You want to start off slowly and gently, the way you'd get up in the morning if you didn't have kids, and put off thinking about what to do for Christmas for a while longer.

But you do have kids. And they're already poring through catalogues, making their lists and counting the days. How can you convince them Christmas isn't just one day, and help them relax and enjoy the whole season? Our solution is to ease into Christmas with some of the following traditions.

Anticipation Chain - *The days will fly by all too fast for you, but kids love something they can hold in their hands and use to count "how many more days 'til Christmas."*

* Cut paper for a simple link chain (pg. 28)

* Number strips 1 to 24 and put them in order. If you have time, write a special message or event (Dec. 21 - school concert) on each link before you stick it together.

* Starting December 1, have your kids remove one link a day. They'll quickly see that the length of chain is the number of days left 'til Christmas.

Count-the-days Cookies - *Fun for lunches.*

* Make or buy plain cookies.

* Spread out and number from 1 to 24.

* Use tube frosting or drizzle the numbers on with homemade frosting on a spoon.

* Let dry well, then pack and toss in the freezer.

* Take out one a day until Christmas.

Anticipation Bulbs - *Paperwhite narcissus bulbs planted on the first of December will bloom around Christmas with an abundance of star-like white blossoms. As kids watch them grow they'll know Christmas is getting closer. Just don't commit yourself to a due-date for blooming when you're dealing with Mother Nature!*

* **Buy firm bulbs treated for forcing and store them in a cool place until ready to plant.**

* **Fill a container with small stones (marbles will do).**

* **Nestle 5 or 6 bulbs into the stones - fat side down, add water to partially cover.**

* **Place in a cool but light place, turn and water occasionally.**

Advent Wreath - *The Advent season begins on the fourth Sunday before Christmas. It's traditional to light a candle on that day and one more on each of the following Sundays. You can buy or make wonderfully elaborate Advent wreaths - but the easiest one we know starts with four hunks of play-dough and a pie plate!*

* **Form four 4" balls from play-dough or clay.**

* **Arrange them on a pie plate (any kind).**

* **Stick a candle into the center of each ball.**

* **Poke bits of evergreen into the balls porcupine-style.**

* **While you're at it try a mini-wreath with a foil tart tin and birthday candles. (Watch it carefully - birthday candles burn fast.)**

Countdown Candle - *The only thing wrong with an Advent wreath is you "only get to light it" once a week - and kids love nothing more than lighting candles. Why not make a countdown candle you can light every day?*

* Hold a ruler next to a 10 or 12" candle. Make 24 marks with nail polish (24 cms tick off nicely). Can't find the ruler? Just wing it!

* Light the candle and let it burn one notch each day until Christmas.

"How but in custom and ceremony are innocence and beauty born?"
Yeats

Christmas Star Banner *- A Special Edition Tradition - see pg. 70.*

Stir- up Sunday - *In England the Sunday before the first Sunday of Advent is called "stir-up" day - a reminder to "housewives" to stir-up the Christmas pudding! Traditionally, each family member takes a turn having a good-luck stir. If you try our pudding (pg. 88) - who knows? It just might set a share-the-work tone for the rest of the holidays. But if it's just going to stir-up trouble - forget it!*

Christmas is a guest that always comes a month before arriving.

"To perceive Christmas through its wrappings becomes more difficult with every year."

E.B. White

Cards & Wrap

If you feel extraordinarily lucky to find time to send Christmas cards, but wouldn't dream of making them with your kids - now you can. We've come up with cards so easy and fun to make it doesn't matter if they never get sent. Don't despair if you can't find time every year. We think card making works best as a "moveable tradition", anyway.

Start by eliminating envelopes entirely. A Christmas post card or a sheet of folded and sealed paper works just as well. Almost everything you need you'll have on hand or can find in a browse around a stationery store. If you decide to make lots of cards or wrap, an assembly line works for some families (who normally get along!). Just don't expect assembly line results! What you can expect, though, is a sweeping surge of smug satisfaction!!

Christmas Post Card - *Start with a blank index card (available in a variety of sizes). Stamp and address one side and decorate the other with ANYTHING your heart desires! For example:*

* A Christmas seal and a scribble. Nothing beats the charm of a child's drawing, even if it doesn't look like anything. If it's drawn in red and green it will look Christmasy (throw in a few gold stars or sprinkles).

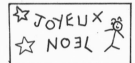
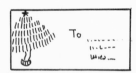

* A finger print design. Press your finger on a stamp pad, then onto paper. Use a fine-tipped marker for details.

* Stickers. Kids favorite. Buy them by the bag in simple geometric shapes to create funny or simply elegant designs. Take your imagination along on a trip to an office supply store.

Simple Self-Mailer - *In line for the simplest Christmas card award is a piece of construction paper folded in three (or half for that matter). Put a design and message on the inside and seal with a Christmas seal or sticker. Inside ideas:*

* Anything that went on the post card will look fine here - drawings, stickers, prints, calligraphy message. Or glue on left-overs and call it a collage.

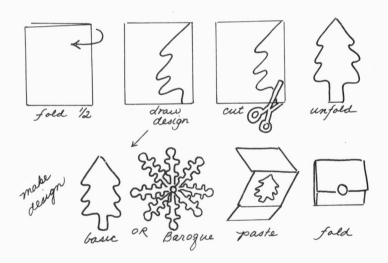

* Cut paper designs are traditional and beautiful. Cut a design out of typing or tissue paper in a contrasting color and paste it in the inside of your card.

Handy Cards

* "Handmade" cards - Have kids trace their hand with a marker or crayon. Special friends and grandparents can save these to compare from year to year.

* Family Hands - Measure the length of the longest hand in the family, add an inch or two on each end. That's the width of paper you'll need. Multiply the width of the largest family hand by the number of family members. That's the length of paper you'll need. (This is not a trick question!) Have each member press his/her/its hand/paw into poster paint or ink pad and stamp onto paper.

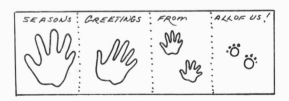

Vegetable Dips - *You can dip almost* **anything** *into poster paint thickened with cornstarch and print it on a card. (Don't tell your kids that -they might try!) Some reasonable things that produce good results are:*

* A potato, carrot, green pepper, onion, stalk of celery - cut in half.

* An apple cut in half - it has its own magical Christmas shape inside.

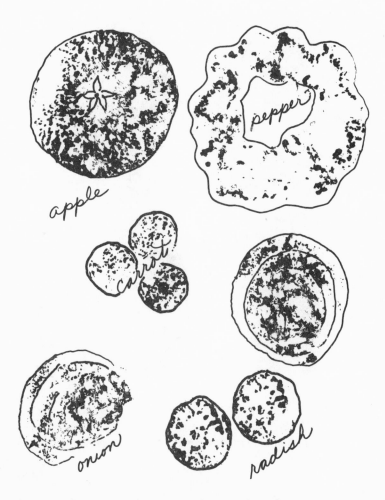

apple

pepper

carrot

onion

radish

Sponge Prints - *Easiest for little kids to work with.*

* Cut a sponge into a traditional Christmas shape - see symbols on pg. 57. Dip in paint, print on paper.

* Try printing in one color, letting it dry, then overprinting (just slightly off) with another color.

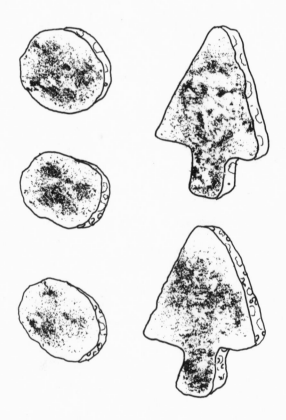

"There are many methods of creating cards which compensate handsomely for lack of ability to paint or draw."

Celebrations

A few more card tricks ...

* Personalized family dolls - fold paper for the number of family members and cut out a doll chain (pg. 30). Draw the faces of family members -note glasses, freckles etc.

Or use some of those photographs from the 2-for-1 sales. Cut out the faces to paste on the dolls.

* Gift of Self - Have each kid stretch out on a piece of butcher paper (you may be tempted to stretch out at this point, but it's cuter if your kids do!). Trace body outlines, then have them draw their favorite outfits and distinctive features on the figures. Roll and send in one of those empty wrapping paper tubes you have lying around.

* Anything from our Christmas tree ornament section that can be put into an envelope or tube makes a very special card-cum-gift.

* This is one card Grandma never sent! Have your kids each do a Christmas drawing on a standard size piece of paper and simply have it run off on a photocopier - or splurge on color xeroxing.

Once those cards start coming in - what do you do with them? String them, hang them, cover the door with them, plasticise them for placemats, line them up on the piano and watch them fall like dominoes every time someone plays...or simply put them in a wicker basket, topped with a bright red bow and keep them in a spot where they can be looked at, touched and appreciated!

Kids who want a container for their own cards can try this:

* Cut a paper plate in half.

* Glue or staple onto a whole paper plate.

* Bend a paper clip to hang it with. Decorate with flair!

P.S. If you never did get those cards you made sent, use them for gift tags, after-Christmas letters, notepaper, etc.

22

Holiday Wrap-Ups

Every now and then an ambitious parent is inspired to make wrapping paper. Consider it carefully. If you simply want to wrap gifts creatively, try these:

* Foil - the easiest thing for difficult to wrap gifts or little kids who wrap with difficulty.

* Saved masterpieces from school - use only with the artist's permission!

* Lunch bags with ribbon handles.

* Green or orange plastic garbage bags - for very large gifts - jazz it up with stickers.

* Wrap loosely with some of the deliciously colored tissue paper available and put in a clear plastic bag.

* Newspaper - comics are fun. Try a Hebrew newspaper for Hannukah gifts.

* Wallpaper, shelfpaper, brown paper bags dressed up with stars or stickers. Tie with brightly colored cord, yarn or lace seam-binding.

* Keep gift in its own carton and decorate with cut-outs from magazines or old Christmas cards.

* Only wrap the cover.

If you want to make wrapping paper as a family project, spread out butcher, freezer, shelf or tissue paper or newsprint and try these:

* Vegetable Prints - as for cards, only more of 'em!

* Spatter Painting - you'll have to spread out newspaper anyway, so make lots! Try placing a leaf or other object on the paper, then spatter paint around it.

* Sponge Prints - as for cards.

If the cards you make demand an envelope, avoid fiddly folding and buy 'em - but buy first and make cards to fit, not the other way around.

Note: Postal regulations on the size of what can be sent:

* smallest: 14 cm x 9 cm

* largest: 25.5 cm x 15 cm

Before the first printed cards in 1843, it was customary for British school children to send decorated scrolls showing their skills in penmanship, composition and art work to family and friends at Christmas. Not a bad idea ...

"The way you celebrate Christmas can be a gift in itself - handing on traditions will give your child a feeling of continuity, comfort, joy in all the Christmases to come!"

Mr. Rogers

Trees & All The Trimmings

A festive tree you decorated together is a symbol of the whole holiday season - you don't really need anything else. Our favorite tree is a mixture of current contributions from family and friends plus mementoes of past Christmases. The ginger-bread man with one eye hangs next to the star you made when you were six, the elegant silver ornament reflects the garish-glazed macaroni angel. Tie it all together with strings of pop-corn and cut paper - it's perfect - it's yours!

Whether you put up your tree a month ahead or not until Christmas Eve, some of your family's most cherished tradi-tions will spring up around it ...

The magical, beautifully decorated tree we know was inspired by Queen Victoria - she must have known a thing or two about pleasing kids - she had lots of them!

A truly great Christmas tree reflects the varying ages, stages, and even the wages of the people who create it!

Stringing Popcorn - *Nothing is more traditional! Put on some Christmas music and -*

* Use a fine but strong needle and thread (or try dental floss).

* Knot the end and start to string popcorn. Alternate with cranberries and raisins.

* Little hands love to roll scraps of foil into balls to thread on for added sparkle.

If popcorn sits overnight it will string without breaking. Even so, unless you have a dog, keep the vacuum handy!

* Short attention spans? Try simply stringing four or five pieces and hang vertically from tree branches.

A tree-trimming party is lots of fun - but it sure makes a mess of the tree!

Paper Link Chains - *You'll be surprised at the attention span of a kid who gets into this. You've heard of art therapy? The simple pleasure of watching a chain of beautiful colors grow in your hands is soothing and therapeutic for parents too.*

* **Cut strips about 3/4'' by 6'' from fairly substantial colored paper. (1)**

* **Form the first strip into a circle and glue together. (2)**

* **Slip the next strip into the link and glue. (3)**

* **Continue for as long as you want.**

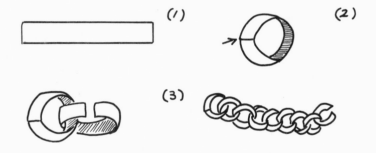

* **You can even buy pre-glued multi-colored strips at a teachers' supply store to be licked into links in minutes.**

* **Don't run all over looking for it - but sometimes stores carry self-stick ribbon which makes super-fast chains.**

Cut-Paper Chains - *A great way to re-cycle old wrapping paper -spectacular made with aluminum foil. You'll feel like a kid again - what more can you ask?*

* **Cut strips of paper about 3" wide by 6" long. (1)**

* **Fold each strip lengthwise. (2)**

* **Cut alternately from each side - almost to edge. (3)**

* **Unfold. (4)**

* **Gently pull each end to open and lengthen.**

* **Tape several together to make a long chain.**

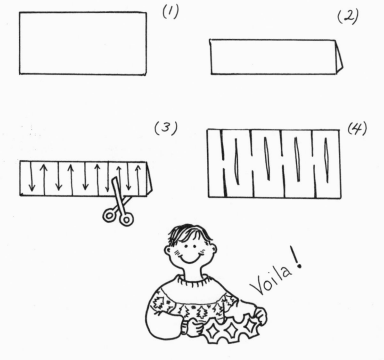

(1)   (2)   (3)   (4)

Voila!

Garlands of Paperdolls - *Charming when cut from comics -sophisticated when sequined and sparkled. Practice with a piece of standard typing paper cut in half. Then experiment with foil, wrapping paper, tissue or parchment.*

* **Fold paper in half (1)**

* **Fold again in the same direction. (2)**

* **Draw figure (extend to edges) and cut out. (3)**

* **Unfold. (4)**

* **A larger piece of paper will fold more often and produce more dolls, but four are easy to work with and a piece of tape will make them into chains.**

* **Depending on your manual dexterity, cut out anything from bears to ballerinas.**

Victorian Paper Fans - *A tree wearing nothing but these is well dressed! Start with an 8" by 10" piece of paper - scraps of wallpaper are nice. Make even fancier fans from doilies - try gold or silver to add a little shimmer to your tree.*

* **Pleat paper into 1" accordion folds. (1)**

* **Fold pleated strip in half. (2)**

* **Tape two pleated sides together in center. (3)**

* **Staple a bow to bottom and insert an ornament hook. (4) (But don't rush out to buy hooks - fans will sit nicely on the branches without them.)**

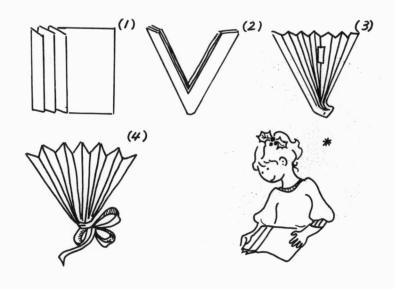

* **Pleating is great for developing hand-eye coordination.**

Christmas Bird - *While you're folding paper, try this delightful bird.*

* Cut simple shape for bird's body from cardboard.

* Slip a pleated strip of paper (see fans) into the slit, then unpleat it and it's ready to nest in your tree.

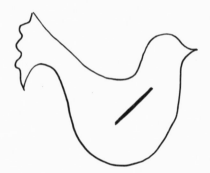

* Suspend a bird over the Christmas dinner table in the Swedish tradition to bring good luck to the household - especially if the traditionally non-participating parent cooks the dinner this year!

* Or make a flock of birds decorated with sequins and glitter.

Cornucopia - *Almost as traditional as the tree. Make them from construction paper, wallpaper scraps, origami paper, last year's Christmas cards or just plain old paper. Decorate with glitter, stickers, bits of rickrack, ribbon, cut paper, doilies and so on.*

* Cut paper into pie-shaped pieces. Experiment with any size, but 6" works well. Or, make a 12" circle, cut in quarters. (1)

* Roll into cornucopia shape, glue along edge. (2)

* Cut a 10" length of ribbon and glue it inside cornucopia on opposite sides to make a handle. (Or use a pipe-cleaner pushed through the paper.) (3)

* Fill with candies, cookies, fruit or nuts. Wrap them first in a square of net material or foil and tie with ribbon, if you like. Hang on the tree.

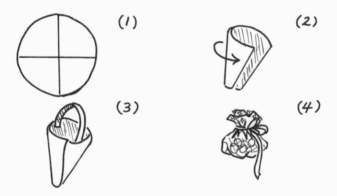

Cone-u-copia - *Brush an ice cream cone with glue and roll it in glitter. Glue on a ribbon handle and fill. Makes a great gift.*

Easy-Squeezy Clip-Ons - *Make these in a pinch with squeeze-type clothes pins. Cut pictures from Christmas cards or make your own Christmasy shapes and glue them on the clothes pins.*

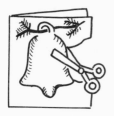

When you take down the tree, don't forget the birds. Hang your popcorn/cranberry strings outside.

Easy-As-Pie Angel - *Perfect to top off your tree. An aluminum pie plate is an easy substitute for the tin pioneers pounded with hammer and nail to make decorations. But the results are just as magical - and even little hands can do it.*

* Cut the edging from an aluminum pie plate. (1)

* With marker (it wipes off) draw a circle and line. (2)

* Place plate on poking surface - try a folded towel.

* Poke pattern (no hammer necessary) with nails, thumbtacks, toothpicks, pins - use a variety of sizes. Draw poke pattern first or just improvise. (3)

* Cut on heavy lines. (4) Fold wing tip into slot A. (5)

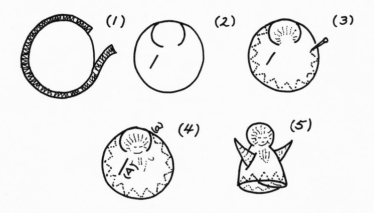

Try tart-size pans for more tree decorations.

* Punch hole for thread or ribbon. Look for the sparkle when the Christmas tree lights shine through!

7

Pipe-cleaner Candy Canes - *Not even vaguely Victorian, but they're cheap, colorful, creative, sugar-free, and you don't have to clean up after them - so who cares?*

* **Twist a red and a white pipe-cleaner together. Bend into candy cane shape. Fini!**

* **Don't forget to show your kids the little pipe-cleaner dolls and animals you used to make as a kid - hang them, too.**

Additional Hang-Ups - *If you don't have enough hang-ups already, try old jewelry (clip-on earrings), sea shells, pine cones, ribbon bows, or some of the "treasures" in other sections of this book - Cinnamon Butterflies, Sachets, decorated cookies, salt dough ornaments etc.*

"Giving, in the form of food and welcome, is one of the most basic pleasures of Christmas."

The Life Book of Christmas

Making Gifts

If you're like us, there are some people you find impossible to buy for at Christmas. There is a solution. It's one of the oldest and best Christmas traditions. Make something with your kids. But before you throw this book down in disgust, let us assure you we're talking about easy "somethings". In fact, the ideas we've selected range from just plain easy to exceptionally easy to embarassingly easy - and we've never had anyone exchange them !

We could go on and on about how personal, creative and thrifty making gifts can be, but why waste the time? You could all be sipping mulled cider with your feet up, cookies cooling on the counter, about the time you'd be battling your way home from an afternoon of shopping.

Stuffed Dates - *These no-bake, old-fashioned treats must have been invented by someone who couldn't stand kids messing around with bowls, beaters and batter.*

* **Fill pitted dates with cream cheese. Top with walnut, pecan or cherry pieces.**

* **Add grated orange or lemon rind to the cream cheese first if you want to be fancier.**

* **To keep kids busy longer, let them roll the finished dates in icing sugar.**

Variations: Fill dried apricots or prunes instead of dates. Try peanut butter as a stuffing.

Spiced Cocoa Mix - *A kid who loves to stir can mix this forever - no harm done.*

> 2 cups unsweetened cocoa
> 2 cups packed brown sugar
> 4 tsp ground cinnamon
> 1 tsp ground cloves
> 3 tsp finely grated orange rind (skip this if you
> can't find the grater)

* **Mix well, pack in jars or airtight containers.**

* **Include these serving instructions when giving: For 1 serving, mix 4 tsp cocoa with 2 tsp milk in the bottom of a mug, fill with hot milk to taste.**

* *For someone special, give a set of mugs with this comforting, aromatic mix.*

Popcorn - *Yes popcorn! What could be easier? A great gift for a favorite babysitter. What's more, corn is the traditional symbol of peace and plenty.*

* **Just pop it, butter it, cool it. Try variations and give some of each.**

* **Wrap in a clear plastic bag and put your gift tag on the twist tie. Slip the whole thing into a brown paper lunch bag your kids have decorated. Tie a ribbon around it - if you have any, and if there's time ...**

Variations: Savory Popcorn - sprinkle on chili or curry powder or dried Parmesan cheese to taste, along with butter.
Pizza Popcorn - add Parmesan cheese, dried basil, oregano and garlic powder.

Nut Crackle Corn - *Watch out. This could get gobbled up before you have a chance to give it!*

> 10 cups popcorn
> 1 cup peanuts, almonds, pecans, or a combination
> 1/2 cup butter or margarine
> 1 cup brown sugar
> 1/4 cup honey
> 1 tsp vanilla

* **Mix popcorn and nuts in a large bowl.**

* **Melt butter, stir in sugar and honey. Bring to a boil then cook gently 5 minutes.**

* **Stir in vanilla, pour over popcorn and nuts. Mix well.**

* **Spread on a foil-covered baking pan and bake at 250° for 1 hour, stirring once or twice - when you remember.**

* **Cool, peel off foil.**

Nutcracker Sweets - *An all-time favorite. Disgracefully easy!*

        1 egg white
        2 cups walnut or pecan halves
        1/4 cup sugar
        1 tsp ginger
        1 tsp cinnamon
        1/2 tsp nutmeg
        1/4 tsp ground cloves
        pinch of salt

* Beat egg white with 1 Tblsp cold water in a bowl until frothy but not stiff.

* Stir in nuts, mix to coat.

* Mix sugar and spices, sprinkle over nuts.

* Bake on foil-covered baking pan at 300° for 1/2 hour. Cool, peel off foil.

Variation: Hot Nuts - omit sugar, coat nuts with beaten egg white, sprinkle nuts with a mixture of 2 tsp curry powder, 1/2 tsp cumin, 1/2 tsp cinnamon, 1/4 tsp cayenne, pinch of salt. Bake as above.

Snappy Turtles - *Who ever said turtles are slow? You won't believe how speedy these are to make - and your kids will be amazed these don't have to be store-bought.*

> pecan or walnut halves - 2 for each turtle
> caramels, individually wrapped kind - 1 for each turtle
> chocolate chips - a few for each turtle

* Place nut halves in twos with a caramel on top on a greased cookie sheet. Heat in oven at 325° for about 5 minutes - just until caramels soften.

* Remove from oven, flatten caramels slightly with back of a spoon (greased), place chips on top.

* Return to oven for a minute to soften chips. Remove, spread chips evenly.

* Chill until hardened, store in a cool place.

Almond Bark - *Better with each bite! Couldn't be easier - and costs much less than the kind that comes ready-made in a box. Older kids like to make this themselves for their teachers.*

* Toast 3/4 cup slivered or whole almonds in a 9 x 13" baking pan at 350° for 5 - 10 minutes.

* Meanwhile melt 16 oz chocolate (semi-sweet or white) in double boiler over hot, not boiling, water, stirring until smooth.

* Pour chocolate over almonds, spread evenly, chill until hardened, break into pieces, store in a cool place.

Turkish Delight - *A traditionally special Christmas candy, with an exotic name that conjures up mystery and magic.*

> 28 g box of unflavored gelatin
> 1/2 cup cold water
> 2 cups granulated sugar
> 1/2 cup hot water
> grated juice and rind of 1 orange and 1 lemon
> red or green food coloring

*   Soften gelatin in cold water. Mix sugar and hot water, bring to a boil, add gelatin. Cook gently for 20 minutes.

*   Remove from heat, add juices, rind and food coloring.

*   Pour into a 8 x 8'' pan which has been wet with cold water. Chill until firm, then cut in small squares, using a knife dipped in hot water.

*   Store in a cool place, loosely covered, for a couple of days. Roll in icing sugar before giving.

Why does the Christmas season always come when the stores are at their busiest?

Flavored Butters

Easy does it! Creaming butter is a good job for kids with energy to burn - you can finish it in the food processor or blender if they burn out.

Honey Butter - *Remember this? Wonderful on toast, muffins, pancakes - whatever.*

> 1 cup butter
> 1/2 cup honey
> cinnamon, nutmeg, grated orange or lemon rind

* Cream butter and honey well.

* Flavor as you like.

* Pack in gift containers and refrigerate.

A gift from your kitchen is always in good taste!

Garlic Butter - *Give this with a French stick or a loaf of Italian bread.*

>1 cup butter
>2 cloves garlic, minced (or 1/4 tsp powdered garlic)
>1/4 tsp paprika
>1/2 tsp oregano
>1/2 cup dried Parmesan cheese

* Cream together butter, garlic, seasonings and cheese.

* Pack in gift containers and refrigerate.

* To use: Slice bread and spread with mixture on both sides of each piece. Wrap in foil and heat at 350° for 20 minutes.

Date Butter - *A real treat with muffins.*

>1 cup pitted dates
>1/2 cup orange juice
>1/4 tsp cinnamon
>grated rind of 1 orange
>1 cup butter

* Cook dates in orange juice with cinnamon and orange rind until soft - about 10 - 15 minutes.

* Stir until smooth, beat in butter.

* Pack in gift containers and refrigerate.

Preserves

Everyone knows what terrific gifts homemade preserves are, but if all you preserved last summer was your sanity - by sitting in the sun - don't worry. There's still time for these.

Pineapple Apricot Conserve - *Easy to make, but takes awhile to cook - your chance to get something else done! Kids can decorate jar labels while it simmers.*

> 2 cups dried apricots
> 19 oz (540 mL) tin of crushed pineapple in own juice
> juice and grated rind of 1 orange and 1 lemon
> 1/2 cup sugar (or to taste)
> 1/2 cup slivered almonds

* Cook apricots in 2-1/2 cups water, covered, until soft - about 40 minutes. Mash.

* Add pineapple (don't drain), orange and lemon rind and juice, sugar. Simmer for 15 minutes longer.

* Stir in nuts.

* Ladle into jars and store in fridge or freezer (leave room at top of jar for expansion).

Raisin Chutney - *Fantastic! Hot stuff for curry lovers!*

> 2 cups raisins
> 2 Tblsp chopped fresh ginger (or 1 tsp powdered ginger)
> 1/2 tsp cayenne
> 1/2 tsp salt
> 1/2 cup water
> 1 Tblsp brown sugar
> juice of 1 lemon

* Whirl all ingredients in blender or food processor until smooth.

* Pack in gift containers and refrigerate.

Cranberry Conserve - *A Christmas classic. See page 86.*

What can you give to the kid who has everything?
Time, traditions, magic and memories.

Crafty Gifts

Does it seem like everyone but you is creating wonderful hand-crafted gifts, while your last year's uncompleted Christmas project is gathering dust in a closet? Then you need one of our easy crafty gifts. They satisfy the urge to create, but are finished in an hour.

Sachets - *Make old-fashioned bundles of scent for drawers and cupboards, but don't bother to sew a stitch. No extra wrapping needed either.*

* **Indulge! Buy bits of all the gorgeous Christmas fabric available - .2 m will make 6 sachets.**

* **Cut fabric into 6'' circles (about) with pinking shears.**

* **Spoon about 1 Tblsp of potpourri or bath salts into the center.**

* **Tie snuggly with narrow ribbon or fancy cord and attach a gift tag. Done!**

Terrific used as a bow on a special package.

Cinnamon Butterflies - *You needn't get all a-flutter when friends arrive bearing unexpected gifts if you've a supply of these on hand.*

* Take three cinnamon sticks (buy in bulk for price, and also so you can choose similar sizes) and glue them together one on top of another.

* Let dry completely.

* Tie with plaid ribbon - 1'' wide looks great.

* Store on your own tree - they'll do double duty as decorations.

Handmade Soaps - *The more kids knead the dough, the better the results.*

* Put 5 Tblsp warm water in a bowl with a few drops of food coloring.

* Gradually stir in about 2 cups of Ivory Snow. Squeeze and knead thoroughly. Add more water if necessary - it should be like play-dough -not sticky.

* Shape into balls. Or press dough into a mold, but line it with plastic wrap first for easy removal. Or pat dough flat and cut out simple shapes with a cookie cutter. Best of all let kids do their own thing.

* Set the soaps aside in a cool, dry place, uncovered, to dry and harden for a day or two.

In the 1880 s soap-bubble parties were a favorite Yuletide pastime - good clean fun!!

Glitter Balls - *Kids love to use glitter - here's the perfect chance.*

*   Buy basic, shiny Christmas balls in bright colors, and contrasting glitter.

*   Hold ball by the top and draw a design on it with clear-drying glue. (Use a fine-tipped brush or a toothpick.) Don't worry about being artistic -free form swirls look terrific!

*   Lightly roll the ball in glitter, trying not to squash the design. Or, just hold it over the bowl and let kids snow glitter down on it. Cover all glue with glitter.

*   Let the balls dry thoroughly.

Variations: Little kids may find it easier to cover the balls completely with glue and glitter. Older kids might like to try making designs with sequins.

More Gift Ideas

*   Check other sections of this book for more good gifts - cards, wrap, tree trimmings, decorations, cookies and so on.

*   A Special Edition Tradition makes an excellent gift from one family to another.

*   Something from Time-Release Recipes would make a great host or hostess gift.

*   Parents on your list would love a copy of this book!

Presenting Your Homemade Gifts

Whoever said the manner of giving is worth more than the gift must have been out shopping for clever containers for homemade gifts. Even a cheap basket isn't cheap anymore! So here are the most practical but effective ways we've found to package gifts.

* Foil bakeware - relatively cheap but festive looking, comes in all shapes and sizes. Cover with clear plastic wrap, top with a bow.

* Holiday decorated paper plates and boxes - every year these become more widely available. Check card shops, grocery stores, bakers' supply stores.

* Plastic berry, mushroom or tomato baskets - line with doilies to spruce them up, or weave with pretty ribbon.

* Glass jars - save all shapes and sizes (if they have re-useable lids) during the year. Add decorated labels.

* Coffee cans - cover with left-over wallpaper, contact paper, fabric etc.

* Baskets, decorated tins, bakeware (glass, aluminum, ceramic etc.), clay flower pots, fancy canning jars, plastic kitchen ware, freezer containers, mugs, cookie jars etc. - all terrific if you find a good deal. Watch for sale items all year.

* A bit of ribbon and a sprig of pine or holly add a special touch to any gift.

* A sampling of some of the things you've made makes an attractive package.

Stumped on Stocking Stuffers?!?

RAISINS · BATTERY · NOTE BOOK · FLASHLIGHT · TOOTH PASTE · COIN · LITTLE BOX OF CEREAL · TOOTH BRUSH · DIARY · CHOCOLATE SANTA · MITT · good old-fashioned orange · TRADITIONAL WALNUT · YO-YO · CRAYONS OR CHALK · CANDY · COINS · SOCKS · BALLOONS

*"It is not necessary to have
expensive or elaborate gifts,
just so they look knobby
and mysterious."*
Celebrations

Inside Tips

Tips On Working With Kids - or -
If this is fun why am I gritting my teeth?

* *If you don't mind muddling through the rest of the year, why suddenly try to be the perfect parent at Christmas? It's like touching your elbow to your ear. Sounds easy but it can't be done! Devote your energy to the things that can be done.*

* *Treat your kids as if they were somebody else's and lower your expectations! Kids aren't perfect either - particularly at Christmas.*

* *Nothing saves time and tension like having the tape, scissors, markers, glue (clear-drying kind), paper, fabric scraps, sparkles, stickers, whatever - all in one place. Keep them together in a cardboard box and store it up high between craft sessions.*

* *Work in stages with a good break in between. If your kids are tired or hungry (or both) - forget it!*

* *For older kids, set things up so you're working separately - together. (How would you like to make something with your mother or father at your elbow, constantly offering well-meant but unsolicited advice?)*

* *Kids will find cooking easier if you assemble all ingredients first, then put each away as used. That way you'll know if you're out of something before you start, and you'll have half the clean-up done.*

* *If you're doing Christmas-making after school or work, plan a freezer or take-out dinner so you're not swamped with having to produce dinner too.*

* *Don't worry about how a completed item should look. Making or doing is lots more important than the end result.*

* *If you really, really care how something is going to turn out, do it yourself. A Bûche de Noël made by kids will look like a Bûche de Noël made by kids! (Of course, if that's better than what you can make, have your kids do it!)*

* *Be pleased with the unusual rather than expecting conformity. Anything kids make is important.*

* *Praise, praise, praise!*

Recipe Notes

* *The recipes in this book haven't been triple tested by professional home economists in designer kitchens. But they have been made over and over again, under everyday conditions, by parents and kids. Some of them kitchen wizards - but some of them kitchen klutzes. And the recipes still work!!!*

* *We haven't indicated how much a recipe will yield - that depends on who's making it, when, and how hungry they are...*

* *There may be more sugar and chocolate in some recipes than you'd normally use - live it up - Christmas comes but once a year!*

* *We use semi-sweet chocolate and unsweetened cocoa - but substitute carob or carob powder in any recipe if you want.*

* *Eggs called for are large, coconut is the unsweetened, dessicated kind, butter or margarine should be softened to room temperature.*

* *Improvise - use what's on hand. That's how great culinary discoveries are made.*

---

* *Being basically traditional, we still use imperial measurements, but if you've switched to metric (pat yourself on the back) or want your kids to learn, here are the accepted (but not quite exact) equivalents.*

1 cup	*- 250 mL*	*1 Tblsp*	*- 15 mL*
1/2 cup	*- 125 mL*	*1 tsp*	*- 5 mL*
1/4 cup	*- 50 mL*	*1/2 tsp*	*- 2 mL*
		1/4 tsp	*- 1 mL*
2 cups	*- 500 mL*		
4 cups	*- 1000 mL*		

Christmas Symbols

The traditional symbols of Christmas for the most part lend themselves to simple designs. Use these for inspiration for cookies or printmaking.

These are a bit more complicated - use as stepping stones to decorating gift tags, labels, cards, windows etc. Avoid wise-men, teams of reindeer, cathedrals - unless you're a kid - in which case anything you make is charming!!

"If you want to see what children can do — stop giving them things."

Norman Douglas

Cookies - Fast & Festive

What's more traditional than making cookies with your kids at Christmas? The shattered fantasy of how much fun it's going to be, that's what! It doesn't have to be - here's a collection of the fastest, easiest cookies around - because at Christmas you have even less time to bake than usual, and kids are more energized than ever.

Of course there are hundreds of wonderful recipes for Christmas cookies from all over the world, and if you've got the time, skill and inclination to make them - great! But we've found the following recipes are all we ever need to produce very credible Christmas cookies. They're old - fashioned, old favourites, old faithfuls.

Short-cut Shortbread - *If it's just not Christmas to you without shortbread, this is the quickest way to get some - no rolling and cutting!*

> **1 cup butter**
> **1/2 cup icing sugar**
> **2 cups flour**

* **Cream butter with sugar until fluffy, work in flour with your hands (kids love to do this).**

* **Press dough with lightly floured hands into an ungreased 9 x 9'' square pan.**

* **Prick dough all over with a fork, right to the bottom.**

* **Bake at 300° for about 45 minutes, until set and golden.**

* **Cut in squares while still warm.**

* **Even better if ripened a couple of weeks in a cookie tin at room temperature. Keeps well - under lock and key!**

Variation: *Try brown sugar instead of icing sugar.*

Toffee Frost-ease - *A recipe that's asked for more than any other -and our preferred way to fill the cookie plate at Christmas.*

1 cup butter
1 cup brown sugar
1 tsp vanilla
2 cups flour
1 cup walnuts, chopped
1 cup semi-sweet chocolate chips

* Cream butter, sugar and vanilla. Stir in flour and nuts and mix well.

* Pat into an ungreased 9 x 13'' baking pan, bake at 350° for 15 - 20 minutes, until lightly browned.

* Remove from oven and sprinkle chocolate chips evenly over top. After about 5 minutes they'll be soft - then spread evenly.

* Cut in squares while still warm.

Peanut Butter Mandatory Munchies - *We know, we know, this recipe has been around forever. But kids never seem to tire of these.*

1 cup peanut butter
1/4 cup honey (or to taste)
1/2 cup skim milk powder
1 tsp vanilla
1/2 cup raisins
1/2 cup coconut
1/2 cup chocolate or carob chips

* Mix all ingredients.

* Shape into small balls, adding a few Tblsp milk if mixture is too dry, more peanut butter if it won't hold together.

* Roll in coconut or sesame seeds.

Basic Ice-Box Cookies - *Pillsbury didn't invent these - but your great-grandmother just might have.*

>1 cup butter or margarine, or a mixture
>1 cup brown sugar
>2 eggs
>2 tsp vanilla
>3- 3-1/2 cups flour
>2 tsp baking powder
>1/2 tsp salt

* Cream butter with sugar, beat in eggs and vanilla, add dry ingredients. Mix well.

* Shape in rolls about 2" in diameter, wrap and refrigerate several hours, overnight, or several days. This makes a fairly soft dough - chill it before shaping if you like.

* In a hurry? Put rolls in freezer for about an hour. (If you use a margarine that stays soft in the fridge, you may have to do this anyway.)

* Slice rolls 1/8 - 1/4" thick, bake on ungreased cookie sheets at 400° for 8 - 10 minutes.

Variations ...
* *To make a border on the cookies, press the shaped rolls in finely chopped nuts, colored sugar, cinnamon sugar or dessicated coconut before chilling.*

* *Frost and decorate as you like - these are a good choice for putting numbers on for advent cookies (pg. 10).*

* *Vary flavor with almond extract, orange or lemon rind, or your favorite spices.*

* *Add nuts (finely chopped), coconut, candied peel, cherries, raisins etc. -whatever you have on hand.*

Pinwheels - *Ultra easy but so impressive.*

* Make basic ice-box cookie dough. Before chilling, pat or roll half into a 12 x 9 x 1/4'' rectangle (approximately - no need to run for the ruler!) on a lightly floured piece of waxed paper.

* Spread with 1/4 cup jam or jelly, not quite to the edges. Don't use too much filling - it just makes a big mess when you try to roll up the dough.

* Roll the dough up like a jelly-roll, wrap and refrigerate. Repeat steps with remaining dough.

* Slice and bake on greased cookie sheets according to basic recipe.

Snowballs - *Satisfy that hands-on craving. Even kids as young as two or three can help mix and shape these.*

> 1 cup butter
> 1/2 cup icing sugar
> 1 tsp vanilla
> 2 cups flour
> 1 cup nuts, finely chopped

* Cream butter and sugar, add vanilla, work in flour and nuts. Shape in small balls.

* Bake on ungreased cookie sheets at 325° for 18 - 20 minutes.

* Roll in icing sugar while still warm. (You can omit this - but the cookies won't be as good - and you can't call them snowballs either!)

* Flavor improves with ripening - if you can keep them that long.

Variation: Little kids may find log shapes easiest to make - you can curve the ends to make crescents - or just leave them and call them Yule Logs.

Imagination Saucepan Cookies - *You can find more complicated versions of this recipe, but kids can make our adaptation in less than 15 minutes. (And eat them even faster!)*

> 1 Tblsp butter
> 1 cup semi-sweet chocolate chips
> 1 cup butterscotch chips
> 1 cup rolled oats
> 1 cup coconut
> 1/2 cup raisins
> 1/2 cup walnuts, chopped

* Melt butter in a saucepan. Stir in chips and melt over low heat. Stir until smooth.

* Remove from heat and add oats, coconut, raisins and nuts. Cool slightly until mixture starts to hold its shape when dropped from a teaspoon.

* Continue making cookies this way - drop them onto waxed paper covered cookie sheets. Refrigerate to set if you need to - depends how warm your kitchen is. Keep in a cool place.

Variations: Here's where you imagination comes in!

* *Try using all chocolate or carob chips, or all butterscotch chips.*

* *Instead of raisins, try chopped dates or cherries.*

* *Try candied peel instead of raisins, almonds instead of walnuts.*

* *If you're out of nuts, don't worry. Use 1/2 cup more coconut or oats instead.*

* *Out of coconut and oats? Just add 3 cups granola to the melted chips and forget the rest!*

Cranberry Moon Balls - *No bake! And not too sweet, thanks to the tangy touch of cranberries.*

1 package cream cheese (250 g), softened
grated rind of 1 orange
1/3 cup honey
1 cup graham cracker crumbs
1 cup cranberries, fresh or frozen, chopped
1 cup raisins
1 cup walnuts, chopped

* Mix ingredients well, adding more graham cracker crumbs if mixture is too sticky. (Depends on whether cranberries are fresh or frozen.)

* Shape in small balls and roll in dessicated coconut or finely chopped walnuts.

* Store in fridge or freezer.

Variation: For Apricot Moon Balls, substitute 1 cup chopped dried apricots for cranberries, 1 cup semi-sweet chocolate chips for raisins, 1 cup chopped almonds for walnuts.

Ginger Snaps - *A short-cut to the aroma and taste of gingerbread without the work of rolling and cutting the dough.*

> 1/2 cup shortening
> 1/2 cup brown sugar
> 1/2 cup molasses
> 1 tsp soda
> 1/2 tsp salt
> 2 tsp ginger
> 1 tsp cinnamon
> 1/2 tsp ground cloves
> 1/4 cup boiling water
> 2 - 3 cups flour

* Mix together in order given, using enough flour to make a soft dough.

* Pinch off small pieces of dough and shape into small balls.

* Roll in granulated or colored sugar - a good job for kids.

* Bake on ungreased cookie sheets at 375° for 10 - 12 minutes.

Great Big Cookies

Make your favorite drop cookie dough.
For each cookie use 1/3 cup dough and spread
to 1/2" thickness. Frost on a greeting
- wrap individually and tie with a ribbon.

Thimbles - *Also known as Thumbprints, Robin's Nests, Jelly Jewels and who knows what else. But whatever you call them they'll get raves at the cookie exchange. And if your kids have never seen a thimble ... well, what more can we say?*

       1 cup butter or margarine
       1/2 cup brown sugar
       2 egg yolks (beat whites separately)
       1 tsp vanilla
       2 cups flour
       coconut or finely chopped nuts, jam or jelly.

* Mix first four ingredients thoroughly, work in flour.

* Shape in small balls, dip in beaten egg white, roll in coconut or nuts. Place on ungreased cookie sheets and press down centers gently with a thimble or thumb.

* Bake at 350° for 10 - 15 minutes. Cool and fill with your favorite jam or jelly, or cranberry conserve (pg. 86).

Mistletoe Kisses - *In a class by themselves - unforgettable. Kids are fascinated by the magic transformation of ordinary egg whites into cloud-like confections.*

> 2 egg whites, at room temperature, with no trace of yolk in them (this is very important)
> pinch of salt
> 1/8 tsp cream of tartar
> 1/2 tsp vanilla
> 1/2 tsp cinnamon (optional)
> 1/4 to 1/2 cup sugar
> 1 cup semi-sweet chocolate chips
> 1/2 cup chopped hazelnuts

* Beat egg whites until soft peaks form, add salt, cream of tartar, flavoring.

* Gradually add sugar (to taste) while still beating. When mixture becomes glossy and stiff peaks form when beater is lifted out, stop beating and fold in chocolate chips and nuts.

* Drop by teaspoon onto foil-lined cookie sheets. Bake at 250° for 40 minutes.

* Remove from oven, cool 5 minutes, then peel off foil and cool completely. (Bonus - clean cookie sheets!)

* Store airtight - if you have any left!

Variation: Flavor with 1/4 tsp almond extract instead of vanilla, use 1 cup coconut and 1/2 cup slivered almonds instead of chocolate chips and hazelnuts. Top each with half a candied cherry, if you have any.

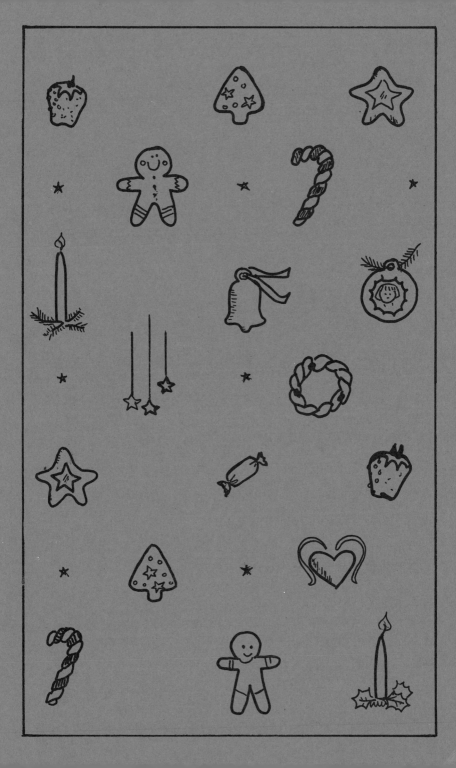

"The challenge is to translate those remembrances of Christmases past into the era of Christmas present - and in so doing perhaps create some brand-new memories."

Betty Crocker

Special Edition Traditions

And now for all those marvelous Christmas traditions you've been avoiding and feeling guilty about because you thought they might be too hard to do. They're not! They just take a little more time than the rest of the things in this book. But they're so much fun to make we couldn't bear to leave them out. So we've broken them down into easy steps - the way we do them.

You won't need to set aside a whole day, just do one step whenever you've got a chunk of free time - usually half an hour will do. Of course Christmas morning will still dawn bright and beautiful if you don't make a Special Edition Tradition, and you won't get a lump of coal in your stocking either. But you just might get a lump in your throat when your kids (who maybe can't get from T.V. to table without bickering) put the finishing touches on a gingerbread house you built together!

Christmas Star Banner - *Specially designed for all parents who can't, won't, or don't have time to sew. Our adaption of the beautiful, hand-crafted fabric advent calendars you see and sigh over in magazines is strictly cut and glue! And while you can use this forever, you only have to make it once!*

You'll need:

> .5 m red felt, for background
> .5 m green felt, for tree shape
> a 30 cm square of yellow felt, for stars
> wooden dowel or curtain rod - about 60 cm long
> .5 m cord for hanging

Time Chunk 1

* Trim red felt to 50 cm by 90 cm.

* Cut green felt into tree shape - 60 cm by 60 cm by 45 cm - as shown.

* Cut 24 yellow stars - 5 cm point to point.

Time Chunk 2

* Turn back a 5 cm hem at top of red felt. Glue down along bottom edge only to make rod pocket.

* Turn up a 10 cm hem at bottom of red felt. Glue down at outside edges only to make star pocket.

* Glue tree shape onto background above star pocket.

* Glue 24 velcro bits onto stars, glue their other halves onto tree.

* Glue 4 velcro bits to inside of star pocket, glue their other halves to background so pocket can be closed.

* Keep little kids busy gluing scraps of felt onto paper - great for cards, gift tags etc.

Time Chunk 3

* Put dowel through rod pocket, tie cord to both ends and hang.

* Store stars in star pocket, put one a day onto the tree during December. Ideally, the last star goes at the top on December 24 ...

Pinata - *A Mexican Christmas tradition that's fun for any Christmas party. Perfect to make with preschoolers because it's messy - and little skill is needed. Start   about a week before you want to use it though, because it takes a few days to dry.*

Time Chunk 1

* Cover a blown-up round balloon with several layers of papier-mâché (strips of newspaper dipped in powdered wallpaper paste mixed with water). Leave an opening at top for filling.

* Hold pinata up to the light to check there are no thin spots, then hang to dry.

Time Chunk 2

* Puncture and remove balloon. Decorate pinata brightly - with paint, tissue paper, feathers, ribbons, stickers, glitter, streamers etc.

* Make two small holes (try using a corkscrew) near top of pinata for a string to hang it by.

* Fill with coins, candies, balloons, stickers, gum, erasers, peanuts in shells, boxes of raisins, folded paper fortunes - anything small but unbreakable.

* Hang pinata where there's lots of room. Everyone then takes a turn trying to break it (blindfolded) with a broom or hockey stick.

* *For a same-day pinata, simply decorate, fill and hang a brown paper bag.*

Marzipan Cookies - *Lots lower in cost and calories than traditional marzipan candies - with delightfully professional results.*

Time Chunk 1

* Make dough and put it to chill.

> 1 cup butter or margarine
> 1/2 cup sugar
> 1 tsp almond extract, food coloring as needed
> 2-1/2 cups flour

* Cream butter with sugar, stir in almond extract and flour. Mix well and divide dough into 3 or 4 parts.

* Add food coloring by drops to each part until you get a color you like. You may have to work it in with your hands. Green, yellow, orange and dark pink will make most fruits and vegetables.

Time Chunk 2

* Mold dough into traditional marzipan shapes you've seen in candy stores. Bake on ungreased cookie sheets at 300° for 30 minutes.

* Use cloves for stems, bits of green dough for leaves.

* Poke texture into oranges, lemons, strawberries with tip of clove.

* Roll strawberries in colored sugar.

Candy Cane and Wreath Cookies - *Produce Christmas shapes without cookie cutters.*

Time Chunk 1

* Make basic ice-box cookie dough (pg. 62) using icing sugar instead of brown sugar and 1 tsp peppermint extract instead of vanilla.

* Tint 1/4 of dough with red food coloring, 1/4 with green, leave the rest plain. Chill - no need to shape in rolls.

Time Chunk 2

* Pinch off small pieces of dough and roll into 1/4" ropes, about 5" long. With a little practice they'll be even and smooth. If the dough is very stiff, working it with your hands will warm it a little and keep it from cracking.

* To make candy canes, put a red rope beside a plain rope on an ungreased cookie sheet, press firmly together, then twist gently. Curve top, sprinkle with colored sugar.

* To make wreaths, put a green rope beside a plain rope, press and twist as above. Pinch ends together in a circle. Decorate with bits of red cherries.

* Bake at 375° for 8 - 10 minutes - don't let them brown. Cool on pan 5 minutes before removing.

Stained Glass Cookies - *Magical, marvelous, one-of-a-kind, original works of art! Guaranteed to please kids - and so much easier to make than we ever imagined!*

Time Chunk 1

* Make basic ice-box cookie dough (pg. 62). Don't bother to shape, just chill it.

Time Chunk 2

* Pinch off small pieces of dough and roll into strips about 1/4'' thick. Use to make outlines on a foil-covered cookie sheet. Pinch ends together well. Start with simple shapes, then try more intricate ones.

* Put brightly colored Lifesavers in a plastic bag and crush with a rolling pin. Use to fill openings in the cookies.

* If you want to hang the cookies on your Christmas tree, thicken dough slightly at top and punch a hole with a straw before baking.

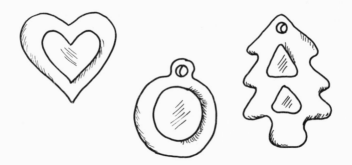

* Bake at 375° for 8 - 10 minutes, until lightly browned. Cool completely, then peel off foil.

* For more ideas, see Christmas symbols, page 57.

Dipped Candles - *Warm glow at a cold time of year - perfect for Christmas or Hannukah. These are pioneer style, but can be made in an hour.*

1 Hour Time Chunk

* Break up a 450g box of paraffin wax into a coffee can. Put can in a saucepan of hot water and heat until wax melts. Add crayon bits for color. (Never boil wax or melt it over direct heat!)

* Remove from heat, cool slightly. Cut a piece of candle wicking or butcher cord twice the depth of the can - this will make a double candle.

* Hold wick in center, then dip it quickly into the wax. Then hold it above can until it cools and hardens. Continue until candle is desired thickness.

* To speed things up, dip candle in a can of cold water between wax dippings.

* Straighten candle by pulling the bottom after each dipping. (It may curl again after next dipping - that's okay - just keep going.)

* Reheat wax as needed - but if it's too hot the first layers may melt off. Add more wax when the level gets too low for dipping.

dipped once   dipped often

* When candle is finished but wax is still soft, roll it on a hard surface to smooth it if you like. Flatten bottom, cut wick. (These candles burn quickly.)

Salt Dough Ornaments - *Easy, cheap, fun - and a breeze for kids with a background in play-dough.*

1 Hour Time Chunk   *(Baking will take longer.)*

        2 cups flour
        1 cup salt
        1 cup water

* **Knead all ingredients with hands. Takes 7 - 10 minutes, so whistle while you work.**

* **Roll out dough about 1/8" thick.**

* **Use cookie cutter or cut freehand (see Christmas symbols pg. 57). Mark details with toothpick or knife.**

* **Poke a hole 1/4" from top with a straw.**

* **Bake on ungreased cookie sheet at 300° about 1 hour - until completely hard and dry.**

* **Remove from sheet and cool.**

* **Decorate with colored markers, nail polish or simply coat with spray varnish (parents only).**

Tips

* **Dough dries quickly so only uncover as much as you need at one time.**

* **You can tint dough by adding food coloring to the water.**

* **If you're after perfection, smooth rough edges with an emery board or light sandpaper after baking.**

* **To make hair, beards, straw etc. use a garlic press - worth buying even if you never press garlic.**

Pretty-as-a-Picture Hang-Ups - *Developed as a way to display those school photos that always seem to be left over after we're persuaded to "buy the package".*

* **Roll out salt dough about 1/8" thick.**

* **Use a juice glass to cut a circle.**

* **Cut face from photo in a circle slightly smaller than the juice glass.**

* **Place photo in center of salt dough circle.**

* **Fold edge over picture, crimp or press down with a fork, poke hole to hang.**

* **Bake at 300° - yes, picture and all - until hard, about 1 hour.**

* **Write name and date on back with marker.**

Super-Simple Gingerbread House - *A classic case of the whole being greater than the sum of the parts. Think of it as just cookie dough held together with frosting glue - it's not nearly so intimidating! Start with our A-frame - after that you'll be on to replicating your own home in gingerbread!*

Time Chunk 1

*   **Make dough and put it to chill.**

1 cup shortening	1 tsp baking soda
2 cups molasses	3 tsp baking powder
8 cups flour	3 tsp ginger
1/4 cup sugar	1 tsp salt

*   **Melt shortening, add molasses and 1/2 cup warm water.**

*   **Mix in dry ingredients slowly - you may not need all the flour.**

Time Chunk 2

*   **For a pattern, use 2 standard size pieces of paper - 8-1/2 by 11" (or whatever it's called these days).**

*   **Use one piece to cut each of two sides of the house. (1)**

*   **To make a pattern for front and back, fold bottom of second piece up as if you were making a square. (2)**

*   **Cut as shown. (3)**

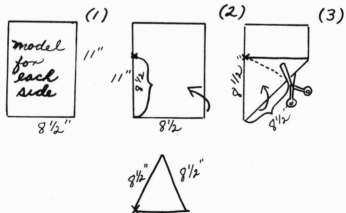

* Roll dough about 1/8'' thick right onto an ungreased flat cookie sheet. Flour lightly so pattern won't stick.

* Cut out around pattern - continue until you've cut a front, back and two sides. To make windows and a door, cut the shapes but leave dough in place.

* Cut scraps into gingerbread people, animals, etc. to decorate outside of house or hang on your Christmas tree.

* Bake at 350° for about 12 minutes. Separate windows and door with a sharp knife, remove when cool. (Use pieces for shutters, chimney etc.) Loosen house pieces carefully with a spatula, then leave to cool and harden overnight (or longer) on a flat surface.

Results, like contact lenses, are in the eye of the beholder!

Time Chunk 3 - *Home, Sweet Home!*

* Make frosting - this is your glue to put house together, fill gaps and cracks, cover mistakes and decorate with.

    4 cups icing sugar
    3 egg whites, at room temperature, with no trace of yolk
    3 tsp vinegar

* Put sugar in mixing bowl, add egg whites and beat with electric beater at lowest speed for one minute. Add vinegar and beat at high speed for 2 minutes, or until stiff and glossy. Keep covered with a damp cloth.

* Cover a piece of cardboard or a cookie sheet with foil to make a base for the house.

* Put house together with frosting glue - pipe it on or just spread with a knife. Have someone hold pieces together lightly while you work. Let it dry until frosting is rock hard before decorating.

* Decorating is up to you and your kids - stick brightly colored candies on with frosting glue - anything goes!

* If you know right now you'll never get around to making this, but are sufficiently motivated to want to, simply use frosting glue to build small houses with graham crackers.

* A gingerbread house makes a great gift from one family to another, from cousins to cousins, from your kids to the hospital children's ward ...

*"In bringing up children
spend half as much money
and twice as much time."*
            Harold S. Hulbert

Time-Release Recipes

Holiday foods are real memory-makers - full of the heart warm-ing, soul-soothing tastes and smells of Christmas. Imagine carrot puddings steaming and cranberries simmering with orange and lemon ... We've gathered a selection of our favorite Christmas recipes that are not only quick to make but can be made well ahead. That's why we call them time-release recipes - because of the extra time they give you right before Christmas when you need it most. Give them a try -then relax and do something fun! You deserve it.

Tourtière -
Wouldn't it be nice to have your Christmas Eve dinner waiting in the freezer so you could devote your energies to being Santa Claus? Traditionally, French Canadians have Tourtière after midnight mass, but serve it earlier if you want to get your kids to bed.

1 lb ground pork	1/4 tsp ground cloves
1 sm. onion, chopped	1/4 tsp nutmeg
1 sm. garlic clove, minced	1/2 cup water
1/2 tsp salt & lots of pepper	1/4 cup breadcrumbs
1/4 tsp celery salt	pastry for a double crust

* Place all ingredients except breadcrumbs in saucepan.

* Bring to a boil and cook, uncovered, 1/2 hour over medium heat.

* Remove from heat, remove 1/4 cup fat, add breadcrumbs.

* Cool and pour into pastry-lined pie pan. Cover with top crust.

* Bake at 400° until golden brown - 45 minutes to 1 hour.

* Serve with chili sauce, pickles & a salad - that's it!

* We usually make several at a time and freeze them, unbaked, then bake from frozen (it takes a bit longer).

Boule de Neige - *A classic French "snowball" which has become a favorite Christmas dessert. Our adaptation can be made in advance and tucked in the freezer 'til you need an X-tra special X-mas treat.*

      1 pint heavy cream, whipped
      1/2 cup chopped walnuts
      1 cup icing sugar
      1 pint any flavor sherbet
      1 pint any other flavor sherbet

* Combine whipped cream, nuts and sugar.

* Line a 1-1/2 quart bombe mold (stainless steel mixing bowl) with whipped cream mixture, leaving a hollow in the center.

* Put in freezer while you stir sherbet to soften a bit.

* Fill hollow with sherbet - one color at a time.

* Cover with foil and freeze several hours ... or days.

* When ready to serve, let sit at room temperature about 10 minutes.

* Turn out on a fancy plate - take a bow!

Cranberry Conserve - *More inspired than regular cranberry sauce, and so versatile. Use it to top a cheesecake, fill tarts, on or in muffins, over ice cream for a fast, festive dessert. Or try it in our Cranberry Coffee Cake.*

> 12 oz bag (about 3-1/2 cups) cranberries, fresh or frozen
> 1-1/2 cups orange juice
> 2 cups brown sugar
> 2 medium apples, peeled, cored and finely chopped
> 1 cup raisins
> juice and grated rind of 1 orange and 1 lemon
> 1 cup finely chopped walnuts or almonds

* Bring berries to a boil in orange juice.

* Add everything else except nuts and bring to a boil again. Lower heat and simmer for 15 minutes.

* Stir in nuts. Ladle into jars and cool. Keeps well in fridge, or store in freezer (leave room at top of jars for expansion).

Cranberry Coffee Cake - *Perfect for Christmas morning. Keep on hand in freezer, then reheat when needed.*

Topping

3/4 cup flour - white or whole wheat
1/2 cup brown sugar
1/4 cup butter

* Mix flour with sugar, cut in butter until crumbs are quite small. Set aside.

Batter

1/2 cup butter or margarine
1 cup brown sugar
2 eggs
1 tsp vanilla
1 cup yogurt
2 cups flour
1-1/2 tsp baking powder
1 tsp soda
1/4 tsp salt

* Cream butter with sugar until fluffy, beat in eggs and vanilla. Stir in yogurt.

* Mix dry ingredients together, add gradually to first mixture.

* Spread batter in a greased 9 by 9'' baking pan.

* Top gently with 1-1/2 cups cranberry conserve.

* Sprinkle topping over all. Bake at 350° for 45-50 minutes.

Christmas Carrot Pudding - *Faster, easier, cheaper and healthier than Christmas cake. Magnificent flamed with brandy for Christmas dinner dessert. Double the recipe for gift giving.*

1 cup grated carrot
1 cup grated potato
1 cup grated apple
1 cup brown sugar
3/4 cup flour
1 tsp soda
1 tsp salt
1 tsp cinnamon

1/2 tsp nutmeg
1/2 tsp allspice
3/4 cup finely chopped suet
1 cup soft breadcrumbs
1 cup raisins
1 cup currants
1 cup chopped nuts

*   Combine carrots, potatoes, apples and sugar, mix well.

*   Stir together flour, soda, salt and spices in a large bowl. Add suet, raisins, currants, breadcrumbs and nuts. Mix well with hands.

*   Add first mixture, blend well. Spoon into a greased six-cup mold. Cover tightly with foil.

*   Set on a rack or tea towel in a pan of boiling water (part way up side of mold). Cover pan tightly and steam for three hours.

*   Or place mold in a baking dish of boiling water (as you would a custard) and steam in oven at 325° for 2-3 hours. For either method, check water level occasionally.

*   Uncover pudding and let cool in mold. Remove from mold, wrap well and store in freezer.

*   Re-steam or simply reheat for about 1 hour before serving. Serve with brown sugar sauce or hard sauce.

*   To flame: Pour 1/2 cup brandy over hot pudding and light.

Brown Sugar Sauce - *Make this old-fashioned sauce a few days ahead and re-heat for serving, or save the job for guests who want to help out in the kitchen. It only takes ten minutes.*

> 3/4 cup brown sugar
> 2 Tblsp flour
> pinch of salt
> 1 cup water
> 2 Tblsp butter
> 1 tsp vanilla
> grated nutmeg, to taste
> 2 - 4 Tblsp brandy or rum (optional)

* Mix sugar, flour and salt in a saucepan.

* Blend in water and stir over medium heat until thickened. (About 5 minutes.)

* Remove from heat, stir in butter and vanilla, sprinkle with nutmeg, add brandy or rum - as you like it! Serve warm.

Hard Sauce - *Softens as it soaks into the steaming pudding - heavenly. A terrific food processor recipe - or do it by hand and vent those Christmas frustrations!*

> 1/2 cup butter
> 2 cups icing sugar
> finely grated orange or lemon rind, to taste
> 2 Tblsp brandy or rum

* Cream butter, add sugar gradually. Beat in flavorings, continue beating until fluffy. Serve chilled or at room temperature.

Rum Balls - *Like parents, these mellow and improve with age! Make them six weeks before Christmas if you like. Then hide them well.*

> 2 cups vanilla wafer or graham cracker crumbs
> 1/2 cup cocoa
> 1 cup finely chopped nuts
> 1 cup icing sugar
> 1/2 cup melted butter
> 1/2 cup rum

* Mix all ingredients in order given and form into small balls.

* Store in a cool place or freeze. Roll in icing sugar just before serving. Best served at room temperature.

* Recipe can be doubled - these make a knock-out gift!

Blender Potato Pancakes - *Latkes are traditional for Hannukah, but these aren't made in the traditional way - they're much quicker.*

> 2 medium potatoes, peeled and cubed
> 1/4 cup milk
> 2 eggs
> 1 slice onion
> 1/4 cup flour
> 1/4 tsp baking powder
> salt and pepper, to taste

* Blend milk, eggs and onion for 20 seconds, adding 1/3 of the potato through the hole in lid while motor is running.

* Add another 1/3 of the potato, flour, baking powder, salt and pepper, Blend 20 seconds more.

* Add last 1/3 potato through hole in lid while motor is running, blend 10 seconds more.

* Heat oil in a frying pan and pour 2-3 Tblsp batter in for each pancake. When well-browned on bottom, turn and brown on other side. Serve with sour cream or applesauce.

"However little one intends to 'do for Christmas', there is no house but the happier for the bringing into it of a little of the Christmas greenery, for with its joyous fragrance comes inevitably something of the blitheness of Christmas tide itself."
"The Delineator", 1920

Atmosphere

When you finally reach those hectic pre-Christmas days what you really want is a festive atmosphere - the halls decked with symbols of the season, splashes of red and green, Christmas music in the air, the aroma of holiday baking filling the house - but still time to contemplate the significance of the season and enjoy the holiday. We try to simplify as much as possible without losing that special Christmas essence. A tall order - but it can be done!

Silent night, holy night
All is calm, all is bright.

Decking the Halls

Clear the decks before you deck the halls. Stuff away the clutter - deal with it after Christmas - or next spring! Fa-la-la-la-la!!

Try these for easy ambience:

* Candles, candles, candles - you can't have too many at Christmas. If you've got brass or silver candlesticks, now's the time to use them - set kids to work polishing. To make candles fit holders well, pack with plasticine.

* Reds and greens - living color! Fresh holly in a silver bowl, pine boughs on the mantle, pine cones in baskets topped with ribbon, pots of poinsettias, cut red carnations or roses, clusters of forced spring bulbs ... Plastic can't hold a candle to such easy, natural splendor.

* Any tree decorations you make can be used around the house too. Try paper-doll garlands in windows, loops of paper chains in doorways, hang a Christmas bird over the table, make a group of foil angels for the mantle, and so on.

* If you have an heirloom-type crèche of pottery or wood, you're all set. If not, you can make a very effective one from salt dough or gingerbread. You'll be surprised how much it will mean to your kids.

* Painted Windows - use poster paint thickened with cornstarch (so it won't drip) to decorate windows and mirrors. Stumped for ideas? See Christmas symbols on pg. 57. To clean off later, spray with window cleaner, wipe with lots of paper towels.

* Snow Painting - send kids outside to decorate Christmasy snow sculptures with leftover paint.

Victorian Kissing Ring - *Pucker up for this quaint tradition!*

* **Cover two embroidery hoops (cheap plastic ones are fine) by wrapping with red yarn or ribbon.**

* **Put one hoop inside the other to form a double ring. Tie or wire a bunch of mistletoe (plastic will do, but fresh is nicer - if you can get it) to the top on the inside.**

* **Decorate with ribbons and bows - hang in a conspicuous place.**

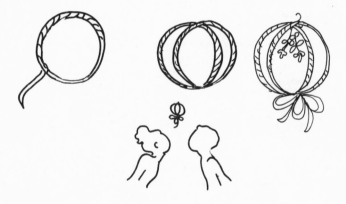

To the ancient Druids mistletoe was a symbol of fertility - so approach with caution !

Door Wreath - *We've yet to find a decent outdoor wreath that's easy and quick to make and doesn't fall apart when you slam the door. (We never said we were perfect did we?) Best to invest in one at a craft fair or shop and keep it forever.*

Cut-Paper Snowflakes - *Evoke special memories - the delicious pleasure of snowflakes melting on your tongue, the magic of unfolding that first cut-paper snowflake in kindergarten. And they're the one sure way to a white Christmas!*

* Start with a square of white paper - experiment with different sizes.

* For a more intricate design, don't stop at four folds.

* This is easier to do than read about. Your kids will need help folding at first, but they'll remember how to do it long after you've forgotten.

Filling The House With Fragrance

Our best memories are often triggered by the sweet, spicy smells of childhood Christmases. Why not give your kids some sentimental scents this year?

Pomander Balls - *Well worth the bit of extra time they take. Keeps kids busy, and the aroma is pure Christmas.*

* Stud lemons, limes, oranges or even grapefruit with whole cloves (buy in bulk). Kids may find it easier to make holes first with a skewer.

* To make pomanders that last for months, the fruit must be completely covered with cloves to preserve it. Otherwise, save time (and cloves!) by just making simple designs.

* Shake finished pomander in a bag with ground spices - cinnamon, nutmeg, allspice - if you like.

* Tie pretty ribbon around pomander for hanging, or place several in a bowl or basket to show them off.

Scent-sational Ideas

* Set out small bowls of potpourri, fill a basket with sachets you've made, use scented candles.

* A gingerbread house smells wonderful. Or try the old real estate trick of just boiling water with spices to get the same effect.

* Cut fresh flowers, forced bulbs. And don't forget pine, spruce, cedar etc. smell fresh and Christmasy when brought into a warm house.

Decking the Table

Cinchy Centerpieces

* Place a fresh pineapple (the colonial symbol of hospitality) on a large plate or platter, surround with pine boughs, holly, nuts, fruit and so on.

* Place candles in hollowed out apples on a plate or pie pan, surround with pine, holly, pine cones - whatever you've got handy that looks good.

* Place votive candles in a shiny, small muffin pan or individual tiny tart tins - if you have any.

* Fill a glass bowl with shiny Christmas balls.

* Fill a glass bowl with cranberries, red and green apples (little kids love to polish them), oranges and lemons, or pine cones and pears -keep looking, you'll find something intriguing.

People used to believe that holly around doors and windows at Christmas would keep witches away - enough said!

Added Touches - No, this isn't just a way to make more work for you. These are jobs for eager kids who "want to help".

* Tie napkins with pretty ribbon -even cheap white paper ones look good this way.

* Make place cards out of gift tags.

* For a really special dinner, make cookie or salt dough place cards.

* Christmas Crackers - place small favors (balloon, wrapped candies, nuts, fortunes, coins, etc.) in cardboard paper rolls (cut large rolls down). Wrap, fringing ends. Plain aluminum foil is easiest -also a good way to use up odd ends of wrapping paper. Tie with ribbon or yarn.

* Kid's Christmas Punch - mix together with water according to directions: 1 tin (250mL) frozen raspberry beverage base and 1 tin (355mL) frozen lemonade. Just before serving add 1 large bottle of chilled gingerale.

19th century Christmas Eve was a carnival of horns, whistles, kettles, etc. -wonder why that tradition didn't survive!?!

Staying Sane

Is this some form of traditional worship before the Christmas tree?!?

No - it's a tension release exercise - which you don't have to change into headband and leg-warmers to do. Simply fall to the floor - nothing will freeze a noisy group of kids into stunned silence like seeing a full-grown woman (or man!) slump to the floor. Slide your hands forward and feel the tension ease from the small of your back to the tips of your fingers. Say ah-h-h-h. Nothing does more for the atmosphere than a relaxed parent.

What do you want your kids to remember? The time you spent shopping and spending, wrapping and sending, scouring and scowling, grumbling and growling - or the calm, contented, creative Christmas you spent together? Relax!

Tranquil Tips

* *Simplify daily life as much as possible. Avoid - like Christmas rush hour - any extra work. Now is not the time to paint the livingroom. Serve light and simple meals.*

* *Just going out for a walk with your kids can relax and refresh everyone. Throw snowballs, make angels in the snow, wander through the neighborhood to see the outdoor lights at night...*

* *Try to avoid a string of over-stimulating experiences and late nights -cranky kids don't make for a pleasant atmosphere.*

* *Try roasting chestnuts just for the fun of it. After all, it is traditional. Cut slits in the flat sides of chestnuts, toss into a pan of boiling water and boil for 5 minutes. Drain. Roast on an open fire, in a hot oven or on a gas barbeque for 15 minutes.*

* *Reading aloud, even if your kids have long outgrown it, can be calming for everybody. Or let one of the kids do the reading. Try the old favorites - The Night Before Christmas, A Christmas Carol, The Bible Christmas story, A Child's Christmas in Wales and so on.*

* Turn out lights, light all your candles and plug in the Christmas tree lights. Sing carols or just listen to Christmas records together. Music can soothe the savage beast - and even a whiny two-year old.

* Remember, nobody's perfect. You will manage Christmas - in your own inimitable way. And that's the only right way.

Merry Christmas!

Need another book?

Order directly from us:

Traditions Press
125 Arden Avenue
Newmarket, Ontario
Canada L3Y 4H7

* **$8.95 (7.95 U.S.) + $1.00 postage & handling**
* **no postage & handling charge on orders over $20**
* **make checks payable to Traditions Press**

Please send

_____ copies of "Making Your Own Traditions-around the year

_____ copies of "Making Your Own Traditions-Christmas

TO:

Name _____

Address _____

City _____

Province/State _____**Postal/Zip** _____

Our books make a welcome... and very easy gift. We'll send them to your friends and enclose a gift card.

Your greeting: _____

Don't hesitate to use the back of this form if you need space for more addresses.

NOTES